CONTENTS ///

For pattern inquiries, please visit: www.go-crafty.com

sawtooth scarf)))

) MEASUREMENTS

Length at top curve Approx 72"/183cm (after blocking)

Depth at center back Approx 8"/20.5)cm (after blocking)

) GAUGE

20 sts and 40 rows to 4"/10cm over garter st. *Take time to check your gauge.*

) NOTES

1 Scarf is worked back and forth in rows. Circular needle is used to accommodate large number of sts. Do not join.

) SPECIAL TECHNIQUE

Provisional cast on

With scrap yarn and crochet hook, ch the number of sts to cast on plus a few extra.

Cut a tail and pull the tail through the last chain. With knitting needle and yarn, pick up and knit the stated number of sts through the "purl bumps" on the back of the chain. To remove scrap chain, when instructed, pull out the tail from the last crochet stitch. Gently and slowly pull on the tail to unravel the crochet stitches, carefully placing each released knit stitch on a needle.

) SCARF

Cast on 361 sts using provisional cast on method.
Knit two rows.
Next row Knit, dec 1 st at end of row—360 sts.

Beg short rows
Row 1 (RS) K186, turn.
Row 2 K12, turn.
Row 3 K11, k2tog, k6, turn—1 st dec'd.
Row 4 K17, k2tog, k6, turn—1 st dec'd.
Row 5 K23, k2tog, k6, pm, turn—1 st dec'd.
Row 6 K29, k2tog, k6, pm, turn—1 st dec'd.
Next row K to 1 st before marker, remove marker, K2tog, k6, replace marker, turn. Cont to work in this way, rep last row 44 times more, end with a WS row—311 sts.

Picot bind off
*Cast on 2 sts, bind off 4 sts; place st from RH needle on LH needle; rep from * until all sts are bound off.

) LACE BORDER

Carefully remove scrap yarn from provisional cast on and place the 360 sts onto the circular needle, ready to work a RS row. With straight needles, cast on 9 sts. K 1 row. Place these 9 sts on the circular needle at the beg of the RS row with the

yarn ready to work the next RS row. With the other end of the circular needle, work border as foll:
Row 1 (RS) K2, [yo, k2tog] twice, yo, k2, k last st of edging tog with the next scarf st—10 sts.
Row 2 Sl 1, k to end.
Row 3 K2, [yo, k2tog] twice, yo, k3, k last st of edging tog with the next scarf st—11 sts.
Row 4 Rep row 2.
Row 5 K2, [yo, k2tog] twice, yo, k4, k last st of edging tog with the next scarf st—12 sts.
Row 6 Rep row 2.
Row 7 K2, [yo, k2tog] twice, yo, k5, k last st of edging tog with the next scarf st—13 sts.
Row 8 Rep row 2.
Row 9 K2, [yo, k2tog] twice, yo, k6, k last st of edging tog with the next scarf st—14 sts.
Row 10 Rep row 2.
Row 11 K2, [yo, k2tog] twice, yo, k7, k last st of edging tog with the next scarf st—15 sts.
Row 12 Rep row 2.
Row 13 K2, [yo, k2tog] twice, yo, k8, k last st of edging tog with the next scarf st—16 sts.
Row 14 Rep row 2.
Row 15 K2, [yo, k2tog] twice, yo, k9, k last st of edging tog with the next scarf st—17 sts.
Row 16 Rep row 2.
Row 17 Bind off 8 sts, k to end—9 sts.
Row 18 Rep row 2.
Rep rows 1–18 until all the scarf sts are attached to the lace border. Bind off.

) FINISHING

Block to measurements, pulling out points of lace border and being sure to keep the curve for the neckline. ■

diagonal scarf ⟩⟩⟩

YARN

⟩ 7oz/200g, 330yd/310m of any
worsted-weight cotton yarn in blue

NEEDLES

⟩ One pair size 7 (4.5mm) needles
or size to obtain gauge

NOTIONS

⟩ Safety pin

⟩ MEASUREMENTS

Approx 7 x 56"/17.5 x 142cm

⟩ GAUGE

18 sts and 24 rows to 4"/10cm over St st
using size 7 (4.5 mm) needles.
Take time to check your gauge.

⟩ STITCH GLOSSARY

Stripe pattern
*10 rows St st, 10 rows rev St st; rep from *
(20 rows) for stripe pat.

⟩ SCARF

Cast on 3 sts and work in stripe pat as foll:
Row 1 (RS) Kfb, k to last st, kfb.
Row 2 Purl.
Rows 3–10 Rep rows 1 and 2 four times—13 sts.
Row 11 (K1, p1) in first st, p to last st, (p1, k1 tbl) in last st.
Row 12 Knit.
Rows 13–20 Rep rows 11 and 12 four times—23 sts.
Note Place safety pin on RS of work. Keep a careful count of the rows to determine when to change from St st to rev St st in the stripe pat.

Rows 21–40 Rep rows 1–20 once—43 sts. Piece measures approx 7"/17.5cm wide (measured along side edge). Cont to work even in stripe pat as foll:
Next row (RS) Inc in first st, work to last 2 sts, k2tog. Work 1 row even. Rep last 2 rows until the long side measures approx 56"/142cm, end with a WS row.
Dec row (RS) Bind off 2 sts, work to last 2 sts, k2tog. Work 1 row even. Rep last 2 rows until all sts have been decreased. Fasten off.

⟩ FINISHING

Block piece lightly. ■

Paul Amato for lvarepresents.com

YARN ①

) 8¾oz/250g, 960yd/880m of any fingering weight bamboo yarn in white

NEEDLES

) Sizes 4 (3.5mm) and 8 (5mm) circular needles each 32"/80cm long *or size to obtain gauge*

) MEASUREMENTS

Approx 14 x 56"/35.5 x 142cm

) GAUGE

22 sts and 32 rows to 4"/10cm over garter st using smaller needle.
Take time to check your gauge.

) NOTES

1 Wrap is worked from side to side.
2 Circular needles are used to accomodate larger number of sts, do not join.

) WRAP

With smaller needles, cast on 340 sts. Work in garter st (knit every row) for 10 rows (5 garter ridges). Turn and place marker to mark RS of work. *Change to larger needles and work 7 rows St st (knit on RS, purl on WS). With smaller needles, work 4 rows garter st. With larger needles, work 7 rows St st. With smaller needles, work 8 rows garter st. Rep from * 3 times more. Change to larger needles, work 7 rows St st. With smaller needles, work 4 rows garter st. With larger needles, work 7 rows St st. With smaller needles work 10 rows garter st. Bind off. ■

Rose Callahan

pocket scarf >>>

❭ MEASUREMENTS

Width Approx 10"/25.5cm
Length Approx 60"/152.5cm

❭ GAUGE

13 sts and 18 rows to 4"/10cm over St st using size 10½ (6.5mm) needles.
Take time to check your gauge.

❭ SPECIAL TECHNIQUE

3-needle bind-off

1 Hold right sides of pieces together on two needles. Insert third needle knitwise into first st of each needle, and wrap yarn knitwise.

2 Knit these two sts together, and slip them off the needles. *Knit the next two sts together in the same manner.

3 Slip first st on 3rd needle over 2nd st and off needle. Rep from * in step 2 across row until all sts are bound off.

❭ POCKET LINING (MAKE 2)

Cast on 20 sts. Work in St st (k on RS, p on WS) until piece measures 3"/7.5cm from beg, end with a WS row.
Place sts on st holder and set aside.

❭ SCARF

Left side
Cast on 32 sts.
Row 1 (RS) *K1, p1; rep from * to end.
Row 2 (WS) K the knit sts and p the purl sts.
Rep row 2 for k1, p1 rib until piece measures 2"/5cm from beg, end with a WS row.
Work in St st until piece measures 6"/15cm from beg, end with a WS row.

Divide for pocket

Next (opening) row (RS) K12, then k20 from pocket lining holder, placing rem 20 sts on st holder for pocket—32 sts.
Work even until lining measures 6"/15cm from opening row, end with a WS row. Place sts on spare needle.
Place 20 pocket sts on needle ready to work a RS row. Join yarn and work in St st until pocket measures 6"/15cm, end with a WS row.
Next (joining) row (RS) K12 from spare needle, holding pocket sts in front of lining sts, *k 1 pocket st tog with 1 lining st; rep from * to end—32 sts.
Work even in St st until piece measures 30"/76cm from beg, end with a WS row. Place sts on st holder.

Right side

Work as for left side to pocket.

Divide for pocket

Next (opening) row (RS) Place 20 sts on st holder for pocket, k20 from pocket lining holder, k rem 12 sts from needle—32 sts.

Rose Callahan

Work even until lining measures 6"/15cm from opening row, end with a WS row. Place sts on spare needle.
Place 20 pocket sts on needle ready to work a RS row. Join yarn and work in St st until pocket measures 6"/15cm, end with a WS row.
Next (joining) row (RS) Holding pocket sts in front of lining sts, *k 1 pocket st tog with 1 lining st; rep from * to last 12 sts, k12—32 sts.
Work even in St st until piece measures 30"/76cm from beg, end with a WS row.

pocket scarf >>> with hood

) FINISHING

Join center seam using 3-needle bind-off method. Sew pocket linings in place on WS of scarf.

Pocket edging

Pick up and k 24 sts along pocket edge.
Row 1 (RS) *K1, p1; rep from * to end.
Row 2 (WS) K the knit sts and p the purl sts.
Rep row 2 for k1, p1 rib until edging measures 1½"/4cm. Bind off in rib. Sew side edges of edging in place.
With crochet hook, work a row of single crochet along long edges of scarf.

Lining

Cut a piece of fabric approx 11 x 57"/28 x 144.5cm. Press a ½"/1.5cm seam allowance to WS of fabric on all edges. With WS tog, sew to scarf along crochet edging on long edges and just above rib on short edges. ■

) YARN 6

) 610yd/560m, 24½oz/700g of any super bulky-weight yarn in periwinkle

NEEDLES

) One pair size 10½ (6.5mm) needles *or size to obtain gauge*
) One spare size 10½ (6.5mm) needle

NOTIONS

) Size J/10 (6mm) crochet hook
) 2yd/2m of fleece fabric for lining
) Sewing needle and matching thread
) Stitch holders

Rose Callahan

) MEASUREMENTS

Width Approx 10"/25.5cm
Length Approx 60"/152.5cm

) GAUGE

13 sts and 18 rows to 4"/10cm over St st using size 10½ (6.5mm) needles.
Take time to check your gauge.

) SPECIAL TECHNIQUE

3-needle bind-off
1 Hold right sides of pieces together on two needles. Insert third needle knitwise into first st of each needle, and wrap yarn knitwise.
2 Knit these two sts together, and slip them off the needles. *Knit the next two sts together in the same manner.
3 Slip first st on 3rd needle over 2nd st and off needle. Rep from * in step 2 across row until all sts are bound off.

) POCKET LINING (MAKE 2)

Cast on 20 sts. Work in St st (k on RS, p on WS) until piece measures 3"/7.5cm from beg, end with a WS row. Place sts on st holder and set aside.

) SCARF

Left side
Cast on 32 sts.
Row 1 (RS) *K1, p1; rep from * to end.
Row 2 (WS) K the knit sts and p the purl sts.
Rep row 2 for k1, p1 rib until piece measures 2"/5cm from beg, end with a WS row. Work in St st until piece measures 6"/15cm from beg, end with a WS row.

Divide for pocket

Next (opening) row (RS) K12, then k20 from pocket lining holder, placing rem 20 sts

pocket scarf with hood ⟫⟫⟫

on st holder for pocket—32 sts.
Work even until lining measures 6"/15cm
from opening row, end with a WS row. Place
sts on spare needle. Place 20 pocket sts on
needle ready to work a RS row. Join yarn and
work in St st until pocket measures 6"/15cm,
end with a WS row.
Next (joining) row (RS) K12 from spare
needle, then holding pocket sts in front of
lining sts, *k 1 pocket st tog with 1 lining st;
rep from * to end—32 sts.
Work even in St st until piece measures
30"/76cm from beg, end with a WS row.
Place sts on st holder.

Right side
Work as for left side to pocket.

Divide for pocket
Next (opening) row (RS) Place 20 sts on
st holder for pocket, k20 from pocket lining
holder, k rem 12 from needle—32 sts.
Work even until lining measures 6"/15cm
from opening row, end with a WS row. Place
sts on spare needle.
Place 20 pocket sts on needle ready to work
a RS row. Join yarn and work in St st until
pocket measures 6"/15cm, end with a WS row.
Next (joining) row (RS) Holding pocket sts
in front of lining sts, *k 1 pocket st tog with 1
lining st; rep from * to last 12 sts, k12—32 sts.
Work even in St st until piece measures
30"/76cm from beg, end with a WS row.
Place sts on st holder.

⟩ HOOD
Cast on 62 sts. Work in St st until piece measures 12½"/31.5cm from beg, end with a WS
row. Divide sts evenly on 2 needles and join
using 3-needle bind-off method.

⟩ FINISHING
Join center seam using 3-needle bind-off
method. Sew pocket linings in place on WS of
scarf. Mark center of base of hood and align
with center seam of scarf. Sew hood to scarf
along long edge.

Pocket edging
Pick up and k 24 sts along pocket edge.
Row 1 (RS) *K1, p1; rep from * to end.
Row 2 (WS) K the knit sts and p the purl sts.
Rep row 2 for k1, p1 rib until edging
measures 1½"/4cm. Bind off in rib. Sew side
edges of edging in place.
With crochet hook, work a row of single
crochet along long edges of scarf and edge
of hood.

Lining
Cut a piece of fabric approx 11 x 57"/28 x
144.5cm. Press a ½"/1.5cm seam allowance
to WS of fabric on all edges. With WS tog,
sew to scarf along crochet edging on long
edges and just above rib on short edges.
Cut a piece of fabric approx 9 x 25"/23 x
63.5cm for hood lining. Press a ½"/1.5cm
seam allowance to WS of fabric on all edges.
Fold in half with RS tog and sew one side
edge seam to fold line, approx 12"/30.5cm.
Place lining inside hood with WS tog and
seam aligned with center back of hood. Sew
in place along edges of hood. ∎

light & airy wrap >>>

Rose Callahan

YARN 🔢

> 5¼oz/150g, 580yd/540m of any fingering weight bamboo yarn in light purple

NEEDLES

> One pair size 10 (6mm) needles *or size to obtain gauge*

》 MEASUREMENTS

Approx 14 x 60"/35.5 x 152.5cm

》 GAUGE

19 sts and 21 rows to 4"/10cm over lace pat after blocking.
Take time to check your gauge.

》 STITCH GLOSSARY

Lace pattern
(multiple of 9 sts plus 4)
Rows 1 and 3 (WS) Purl.
Row 2 K3, *yo, k2, ssk, k2tog, k2, yo, k1; rep from * to last st, end k1.
Row 4 K2, *yo, k2, ssk, k2tog, k2, yo, k1; rep from * to last st, end k2.
Rep rows 1–4 for lace pat.

》 SHAWL

Cast on 67 sts. Work in lace pat until piece measures 58"/147.5cm, end with a WS row. Bind off.

》 FINISHING

Block piece to measurements. ■

LACY WRAP HOW-TO

This lacy shawl employs a very simple four-row eyelet pattern. The only stitches you need to know are knit, purl, yarn over, knit 2 together (k2tog) and slip, slip, knit (ssk). Below we show the ssk in two steps.

1 Insert the right-hand needle "knitwise," or as if to knit, into the next two stitches on the left needle, one at a time. Here we show slipping the second stitch.

2 Insert the left needle into the fronts of these two stitches, as shown, and knit them together. This decrease will slant the stitches to the left.

pastel stripes scarf >>>>

YARN

> 1¾oz/50g, 110yd/110m of any DK weight wool yarn each in light blue (A), light green (B), light yellow (C), light purple, (D) and light pink (E)

NEEDLES

> Sizes 5 and 10 (3.75 and 6mm) circular needles, each 40"/100cm long *or size to obtain gauge*

NOTIONS

> Size H/8 (5mm) crochet hook for fringe

MEASUREMENTS

Approx 4 x 80"/10 x 203cm

GAUGE

16 sts and 30 rows to 4"/10cm over pat st using sizes 5 and 10 (3.75 and 6mm) needles. *Take time to check your gauge.*

STITCH GLOSSARY

Pattern stitch

Rows 1 and 2 With smaller needle, knit.
Rows 3 and 4 With larger needle, knit.
Rows 5 and 6 Rep rows 1 and 2.
Rep rows 1–6 for pattern stitch.

NOTE

Scarf is worked back and forth in rows. Circular needle is used to accommodate large number of sts. Do not join.

SCARF

With smaller needle and A, cast on 308 sts. Beg pattern st, completing the 6 rows of the pattern stitch with each color in the following sequence: A, B, C, D and E. Bind off loosely.

FINISHING

Cut 10 lengths of yarn in each color, each 16"/40.5cm long. With 5 strands held tog, fold fringe in half and using crochet hook, pull loop through one stitch in a matching color stripe. Pull ends of strands through loop. Rep with each color on each end. Trim even. ■

Paul Amato for Ivarepresents.com

ruffled stole »»»

YARN ③

› 7oz/200g, 420yd/390m of any DK weight cotton blend yarn in pink (MC)

› 2⅔oz/80g, 70yd/70m of any novelty weight polyester ruffles yarn in white (CC)

NEEDLES

› One size 5 (3.75mm) circular needle, 24"/60cm *or size to obtain gauge*

› MEASUREMENTS

Approx 7½ x 60"/19 x 152cm

› GAUGE

24 sts and 24 rows to 4"/10cm over pat st using size 5 (3.75mm) needles and MC. *Take time to check your gauge.*

› STITCH GLOSSARY

Garter rib pat

(multiple of 6 sts plus 9)

Row 1 (RS) K4, p1, *k5, p1; rep from * to last 4 sts, k4.

Row 2 (WS) K3, *p1, k1, p1, k3; rep from * to end.

Rep rows 1 and 2 for garter rib pat.

› NOTES

1 Ruffle ribbon yarn is cut at the end of each ruffle row.

2 When working with the ruffle ribbon yarn, work the first and last sts with the end of the ribbon folded over to the inside. Insert working needle into the first two holes together and pull through the stitch on needle. This eliminates a raw edge at the end of each row of ruffles.

Jack Deutsch

› SCARF

With MC, cast on 45 sts.

*Beg with a RS row, work in garter rib pat for 11 rows, end with a RS row.

Next row (WS) With CC , knit.

Without turning work, slide the sts back to the opposite end of needle to work next row from WS.

Next row (WS) With MC, work row 2 of garter rib pat.

Rep from * until scarf measures approx 58½"/148.5cm.

Work 11 rows more in garter rib pat, end with a RS row. Bind off on WS. ■

kid's chevron scarf >>>

YARN

) 5¼oz/150g, 300yd/280m of any worsted-weight cotton and acrylic blend yarn in red

NEEDLES

) One pair size 4 (3.5mm) needles *or size to obtain gauge*

NOTIONS

) Stitch markers

) MEASUREMENTS

Length Approx 43½"/110.5cm
Width at center Approx 5½"/14cm
Width at ends Approx 10"/25.5cm

) GAUGE

20 sts and 27 rows to 4"/10cm over St st using size 4 (3.5mm) needles.
Take time to check your gauge.

) STITCH GLOSSARY

Kfb Inc 1 st by knitting into the front and back of same st.
Pbkf Inc 1 st by purling in back loop, then knitting in front loop of same st.
M1 Insert LH needle under strand between st just worked and next st. Knit this strand, do NOT twist.
SK2P Sl 1, k2tog, pass sl st over k2tog.

) NOTES

1 Scarf is reversible.
2 Incs and decs are worked on both RS and WS throughout.
3 RS and WS reverse at beg of chart 2.

) SCARF

Cast on 55 sts. Knit 2 rows.
Row 1 (WS) K5, [p5, k5] 5 times.
Row 2 (RS) K10, p5, [k5, p5] 3 times, k10.
Place marker on last row worked for RS of scarf.
Rep last 2 rows once, then row 1 once.

Beg chart 1

Work row 1–46 of chart 1–29 sts.
Next row (RS) K10, p9, k10.
Next row K5, p5, k9, p5, k5.
Rep last 2 rows until piece measures 35"/89cm from beg, end with a RS row.
Change marker to mark next row as a RS row.

Beg chart 2

Work rows 1–47 of chart 2–55 sts.
Next row (WS) K10, [p5, k5] 3 times, p5, k10.
Next row [K5, p5] 5 times, k5.
Rep last 2 rows once more.
Knit 2 rows. Bind off. ■

Paul Amato for lvarepresents.com

CHART 1
end with 29 sts

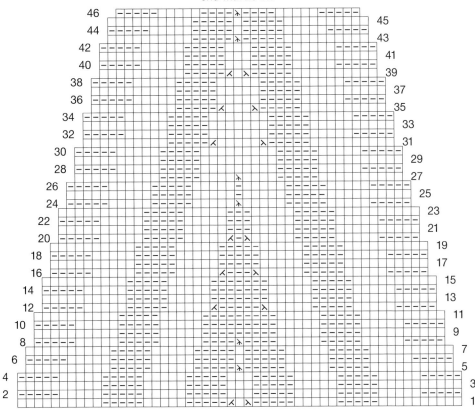

beg with 55 sts

CHART 2
end with 55 sts

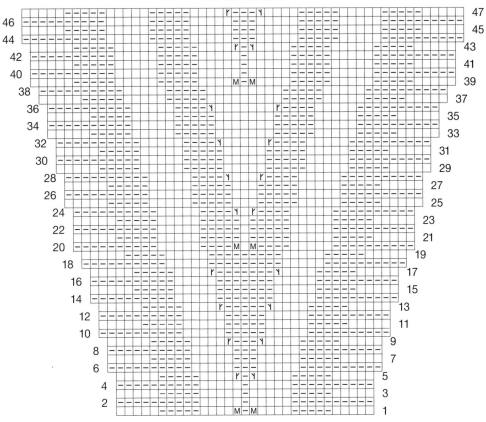

beg with 29 sts

STITCH KEY
- ☐ k on RS, p on WS
- ⊟ p on RS, k on WS
- ⊠ k2tog
- ⊠ SKP
- ⊠ SK2P
- Ⓜ M1
- ⟙ pbkf
- ⟙ kfb

i-cord necklace ⟩⟩⟩

YARN ④

❭ 3½oz/100g, 210yd/200m of any worsted-weight cotton and wool blend yarn in light pink (A)

❭ Small amounts each in red (B) and dark pink (C)

NEEDLES

❭ Two size 3 (3.25mm) double-pointed needles (dpns) *or size to obtain gauge*

NOTIONS

❭ One Boye® Bloom Loom

❭ Optional ribbon approx 18"/45.5cm long

❭ MEASUREMENTS

I-cord Approx ½"/1.5cm x 10yd/9m

❭ GAUGE

24 sts and 29 rows to 4"/10cm over St st using size 3 (3.25mm) needles.
Take time to check your gauge.

❭ NOTES

1 Make blooms first and use remainder of A for I-cord.

2 Blooms can be worked in colors as desired or follow instructions below to replicate sample.

❭ TOP FLOWER

Outer petals

With Bloom Loom, wrap outer pegs following How-To on opposite page, making 3 loops with B.
With A, wrap outer peg for 2 loops.

Inner petals

With Bloom Loom and B, work petals, making 2 loops around inner pegs.

Center stitching

With A, stitch center foll Bloom Loom How-To instructions.
With B, working inside stitched ring, stitch center in same manner.

❭ CENTER FLOWER

Outer petals

With Bloom Loom and B, wrap outer pegs making 4 loops.

Inner petals

With Bloom Loom and A, wrap inner pegs making 2 loops.

Rose Callahan

Center stitching

With A, stitch center foll Bloom Loom How-To instructions.

With B, working inside stitched ring, stitch center in same manner.

❯ LOWER FLOWER

Outer petals

With Bloom Loom and C, wrap outer pegs making only 1 loop.

Inner petals

With Bloom Loom and C, wrap inner pegs making 2 loops.

Center stitching

With A, stitch center foll Bloom Loom How-To instructions.

With C, if desired, make vertical stitches around center stitching, working through the centers of each petal, using photo as guide.

❯ I-CORD

With dpns and A, cast on 6 sts, leaving a long tail. *Knit one row. Without turning work, slide the sts back to the opposite end of needle to work next row from RS. Pull yarn tightly from the end of the row. Rep from * until cord measures approx 10yd/9m from beg. Bind off. Cut yarn leaving long tail.

❯ FINISHING

Coil I-cord into necklace shape at desired length, weaving ends loosely in and out of coil for tangled, casual look. Tie cast-on and bound-off tails tog in a bow to close necklace. If desired, tie ribbon around coil at back of neck to maintain neck opening.

Pin or sew blooms to cord as desired or use photo as guide. ■

BLOOM LOOM HOW-TO

1 Leaving a long tail, anchor yarn in notch at space marked 7. Working around outer pegs, bring yarn across loom to 1 and around peg to 12, then back to 6. Repeat to create the desired number of loops.

2 Next, bring yarn across loom to space 2, around peg to 1, back across to 7 and around peg to 8. Repeat until desired number of loops have been made around peg. Continue to work counterclockwise around loom in this manner.

3 When outer pegs have been wrapped, change color and wrap inner pegs with two loops each in the same manner. Thread tapestry needle with beginning tail and pull it up firmly between petals 6 and 7.

4 Bring needle down through center of loom at 5 and back up at 8. Continue in this manner until the center has been stitched around, as shown above.

spiral scarf >>>

YARN

〉 1¾oz/50g, 20yd/20m of any worsted-weight cotton blend ruffle yarn in white

NEEDLES/HOOK

〉 One pair size 10 (6mm) needles OR size J/10 (6mm) crochet hook *or size to obtain gauge*

NOTIONS

〉 Locking stitch markers

〉 Sewing needle and matching thread

〉 MEASUREMENTS

Approx 4 x 60"/10 x 152cm

〉 GAUGE

11 sts and 15 rows to 4"/10cm over St st/sc using size 10 (6mm) needles/size J/10 (6mm) crochet hook.
Take time to check your gauge.

〉 NOTES

1 Scarf can be either knit or crocheted.
2 If using yarn composed of mesh loops with a ruffled lower edge. To work, insert needle or hook into top row of loops opposite ruffled edge.
3 Optional: In finishing, tack yarn edge to scarf with sewing needle and thread in matching color.

〉 CROCHET SCARF

Note Scarf is worked across 2 sc sts. Markers are placed at the beg and end of each row to keep place.

Insert hook from front to back through 4th loop from end, *insert hook into next loop and draw through; rep from * twice more for ch 3. Turn.

Row 1 Sc in 2nd ch from hook. Fold end of yarn with unworked loops inward. Sc in next ch st, drawing loop through both the ch st and the 1st unworked loop to secure end. Ch 1, turn, place marker (pm) under loops of this ch 1.

Row 2 Sc in next 2 sts (do not count turning ch as a st), ch 1, turn. Pm under loops of this ch.

Row 3 Sc in next 2 sts. Remove marker from last st. Ch 1, turn, pm under loops of this ch.
Rep row 3 until 6 loops rem.

Next row Sc in next 2 sts, remove marker from last st. Ch 1 and cont drawing yarn through loops along top and side edge until ruffle is reached. Pull ruffle end through last loop and secure.

〉 KNIT SCARF

Note Fold over edge at beg of cast on. Always knit into the same side of the yarn, taking care not to twist yarn mid-row. Cast on 3 sts by inserting needle from back to front through 3 consecutive loops. Turn.

Row 1 Insert RH needle into 1st st on LH needle as if to knit, wrap RH needle with next loop in working yarn, draw loop through. *Insert RH needle into the next st on the LH needle as if to knit, skip one loop, place next loop on RH needle and draw loop through; rep from * once more. Turn.
Rep row 1 until approx 6"/15cm of yarn rem. Bind off in pat, drawing one st over the next, to last st. Draw yarn through last st and tighten slightly. ■

Jack Deutsch

diagonal lace scarf ⟫⟫⟫

YARN (3)

❭ 5¼oz/150g, 310yd/290m of any DK weight cotton blend yarn in light green

NEEDLES

❭ One pair size 9 (5.5mm) needles *or size to obtain gauge*

❭ ■■□□

❭ MEASUREMENTS
Length Approx 58"/147cm
Width Approx 9"/23cm

❭ GAUGE
17 sts and 20 rows to 4"/10cm over diagonal lace pat using size 9 (5.5mm) needles. *Take time to check your gauge.*

❭ BACK
Cast on 38 sts. K 3 rows.

Beg diagonal lace pat
Row 1 (RS) Sl 1, [k2tog, yo, k1] 12 times, k1.
Row 2 Sl 1, p to end.
Row 3 [K2tog, yo, k1] 12 times, k2.
Row 4 Rep row 2.
Row 5 Sl 1, k1, [k2tog, yo, k1] 12 times.
Row 6 Rep row 2.
Rep rows 1–6 for diagonal lace pat until piece measures 57"/144.5cm from beg, end with a WS row. K 3 rows.
Bind off.

❭ FINISHING
Block lightly. ■

Paul Amato for kvaropresents.com

lace-edged scarf ⟩⟩⟩

Paul Amato for Varepresents.com

⟩ YARN

⟩ 5¼oz/150g, 250yd/230m of any sport weight cotton blend yarn in pale aqua

NEEDLES

⟩ One size 5 (3.75mm) circular needle, 32"/80cm long *or size to obtain gauge*

NOTIONS

⟩ Stitch markers

⟩ MEASUREMENTS

Width Approx 58"/147cm
Length Approx 27"/68.5cm

⟩ GAUGE

22 sts and 40 rows to 4"/10cm over garter st using size 5 (3.75mm) needle.
Take time to check your gauge.

⟩ NOTES

1 Shawl is worked from center back neck outward.
2 Circular needle is used to accommodate large number of sts, do not join.

⟩ SHAWL

Cast on 3 sts.
Row 1 (inc RS) K1, [yo, k1] twice—5 sts.
Row 2 and all WS rows Knit.
Row 3 (inc) K2, *yo, k1; rep from * to last st, k1—7 sts.
Row 5 (inc) Rep row 3—11 sts.
Row 7 (inc) K2, yo, k3, yo, place marker (pm), k1, pm, yo, k3, yo, k2—15 sts.
Row 9 (inc) K2, yo, k to marker, yo, sl marker, k1, sl marker, yo, k to last 2 sts, yo, k2—4 sts inc'd.
Row 10 Knit.
Rep last 2 rows 75 times—319 sts.
Piece measures approx 22½"/57cm from beg to center point. Bind off.

Upper edge border

Cast on 5 sts.
Row 1 (RS) K to the last st, sl last st, with RS facing, insert LH needle into edge st at left side of upper edge of shawl and k this loop, place this st and slipped st back on LH needle and k these sts tog, turn.
Row 2 (WS) Knit.

Beg chart 1

Working into every other row, cont to join edging in this way, rep rows 1–12 of chart 1 along upper edge, end with a WS row. Bind off.

Lower edge border

Cast on 12 sts.
Row 1 (RS) K to the last st, sl last st, with RS facing, insert LH needle into edge st at upper right edge of shawl (edge of upper edge border) and k this loop, place this st and slipped st back on LH needle and k these sts tog, turn.
Row 2 (WS) Knit.

Beg chart 2

Working into every st, cont to join edging in this way, rep rows 1–10 of chart 2 along lower edge, end with a WS row. Bind off.

⟩ FINISHING

Block lightly. ■

CHART 1

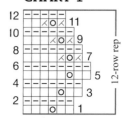

CHART 2

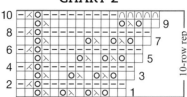

STITCH KEY

☐ k on RS, p on WS	⊠ SKP
⊟ p on RS, k on WS	⊙ yo
⊠ k2tog on RS, k2tog on WS	⊡ bind off 1 st

eyelets scarf >>>

YARN

❯ 5¼oz/150g, 300yd/280m of any
worsted-weight microfiber yarn
in red

NEEDLES

❯ One pair size 8 (5mm) needles
or size to obtain gauge

❯ MEASUREMENTS

Approx 6 x 62"/15 x157.5cm

❯ GAUGE

20 sts and 22 rows to 4"/10cm over lace pat
using size 8 (5mm) needles.
Take time to check your gauge.

❯ STITCH GLOSSARY

Lace pattern
(multiple of 3 sts plus 1)
Row 1 (RS) *K2tog, yo, k1; rep from * to last
st, k1.
Row 2 (WS) *P2tog, yo, p1; rep from * to
last st, p1.
Rep rows 1 and 2 for lace pat.

❯ SCARF

Cast on 31 sts. Work in lace pat until scarf
measures approx 62"/157.5cm from beg.
Bind off. ◼

lacy leaves scarf >>>

Paul Amato for Ivarepresents.com

YARN ③

› 7oz/200g, 440yd/410m of any DK weight cotton yarn in light purple

NEEDLES

› One pair size 5 (3.75mm) needles *or size to obtain gauge*

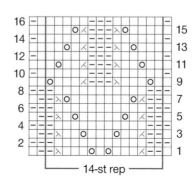

› MEASUREMENTS

Approx 8½ x 56"/21.5 x 142cm

GAUGE

21 sts and 28 rows to 4"/10cm over chart pat using size 5 (3.75mm) needles.
Take time to check your gauge.

› SCARF

Cast on 45 sts.
Set-up row (WS) K1, p6, [k3, p11] twice, k3, p6, k1.

Beg chart

Row 1 (RS) Work first st of chart, work 14-st rep 3 times across, work last 2 sts of chart.

Cont to work chart in this manner until row 16 is complete. Rep rows 1–16 until piece measures approx 56"/142cm from beg, end with a chart row 8.

Bind off row *K2tog, place st back on LH needle; rep from * until all sts have been bound off. ■

STITCH KEY

☐	k on RS, p on WS
⊟	p on RS, k on WS
⊠	k2tog
⊠	SKP
⊙	yo

14-st rep

Rose Callahan

YARN

> 2oz/60g, 150yd/140m of any DK weight wool yarn in bright blue

NEEDLES

> One pair size 7 (4.5mm) needles *or size to obtain gauge*

NOTIONS

> 1 button

> MEASUREMENTS

Approx 7½ x 25"/19 x 63.5cm

> GAUGE

16 sts and 28 rows to 4"/10cm over mesh pat, using size 7 (4.5mm) needles. *Take time to check your gauge.*

> STITCH GLOSSARY

Mesh pattern
(multiple of 2 sts, plus 1)
Row 1 (RS) Purl.
Row 2 Rep row 1.
Row 3 K1, *yo, SKP; rep from * to end.
Rows 4–6 Rep row 1.
Row 7 K1, *yo, k2tog* rep from * to end.
Row 8 Rep row 1.
Rep rows 1–8 for mesh pattern.

> SCARFLET

Cast on 31 sts.
Purl one (WS) row.
Work in mesh pat until work measures approx 25"/63.5cm, and 36"/91.5cm of yarn remains, end with a row 2 or 6. Bind off purlwise.

> FINISHING

Block lightly.
Using guide, attach button so scarflet fits snugly around neck, using mesh eyelet for buttonhole. ■

YARN ④

⟩ Small amounts of any worsted-weight cotton yarn in orange (A), light orange (B), dark pink (C), and green (D)

⟩ Small amount of any lightweight scrap yarn in pale gray (E) for center of flower with leaves

NEEDLES/HOOK

⟩ Size F/5 (3.5mm) crochet hook or size to obtain gauge

NOTIONS

⟩ One pin back for each flower

⟩ MEASUREMENTS/GAUGE

For single color rosette
Diameter Approx 2¾"/7cm
For 3-color flower
Diameter Approx 3"/7.5cm
For flower with leaves
Diameter (without leaves) Approx 2"/5cm
Length of leaf (approx) Approx 1½"/4cm
Take time to check your gauge.

⟩ NOTE

Use colors as desired.

⟩ SINGLE COLOR ROSETTE

Leaving long tail, chain 35.
Row 1 Dc in 5th ch from hook, *ch 1, skip 1 ch, [dc, ch 1, dc] in next ch—V-st made; rep from * to end, turn—16 V-sts made.
Row 2 Ch 3 (counts as dc), 5 dc in first ch-1 space, *sc in next ch-1 space, 6 dc in next ch-1 space—1 shell st made; rep from * 14

Rose Callahan

times more—16 shells. Fasten off leaving long tail for sewing.

⟩ FINISHING

Coil strip to form rosette. Use long tail to sew tog. Sew pin to back. See How-To on opposite page.

⟩ 3-COLOR FLOWER

With desired color for center of flower, ch 5, join with sl st in first ch to form ring.

Rnd 1 Work 8 sc in ring.
Rnd 2 Ch 3 (counts as 1 dc), *2 dc in next sc; rep from * 6 times more, end 1 dc in next sc, with 2nd color join with sl st in top of ch-3. Do not cut first color.
Rnd 3 With 2nd color, ch 1 *sc in next dc, (hdc, 3 dc, hdc) in next dc; rep from * 7 times more—8 petals. With first color, join with sl st to beg ch 1. Cut 2nd color.
Rnd 4 With first color, and working from behind, ch 2, insert hook from back to front

to back around the beg ch-3 from rnd 2 and work 1 sc, ch 5, *skip next dc, work 1 dc around post of next dc in rnd 2 as before, ch 3; rep from * 7 times more. With 3rd color join with sl st in 2nd ch of beg ch 5.

Rnd 5 Ch 1, *(sc, hdc, 3 dc, hdc, sc) in next ch-3 space; rep from * 7 times more, with first color join with sl st in top of ch-3. Cut 3rd color.

Rnds 6 and 7 Rep rnds 4 and 5 with first color, or desired color. Fasten off.

❭ FINISHING
Sew pin to back.

❭ FLOWER WITH LEAVES
Center of flower
With E, make a slip knot so that pulling the tail (and not the working yarn) tightens the loop.

Rnd 1 Sc 1, ch 2, dc 11 in slip knot. Pull tail to tighten loop. With desired color, join with sl st in top of beg ch-2. Cut first color.

Petals
Rnd 1 *Ch 3, skip next st, sl st in next st; rep from * 5 times more, end, ch 1.

Rnd 2 *(Sc, hdc, 3 dc, hdc, sc) in next ch-3 space; rep from * 5 times more, join with sl st to first sc. Fasten off.

Leaves
With D, attach yarn to back of any petal, *insert hook from back to front to back around sl st in rnd 1 and work sc, ch 13, sl st 1 in 2nd ch from hook, [work 3 dc next ch] 9 times, [sc in next ch] twice, ch 2; rep from * until 6 leaves are complete, join with sl st to first st. Fasten off.

❭ FINISHING
Sew pin to back. ▪

CROCHETED FLOWERS HOW-TO

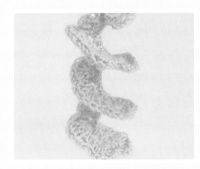

1 When two rounds of the crochet rosette are complete, the strip forms a loose spiral, as above. Tighten the spiral so that there are four layers of petals.

2 Be sure that the tail from the beginning chain is at the center of the widest layer. Thread the needle with the tail and sew the petals in place through all layers.

3 Sew a pin back to the wrong side of the rosette to wear as a brooch.

cozy lace shawl 〉〉〉

YARN ❹

〉 16oz/460g, 800yd/740m of any worsted-weight cotton yarn in variegated blue and purple

NEEDLES

〉 One pair size 8 (5mm) needles *or size to obtain gauge*

NOTIONS

〉 Size I/9 (5.5mm) crochet hook

〉 Stitch markers

〉 MEASUREMENTS

Approx 19½ x 48"/49.5 x 122cm

〉 GAUGE

17 sts and 20 rows to 4"/10cm over St st using size 8 (5mm) needles.
Take time to check your gauge.

〉 STITCH GLOSSARY

SK2P Sl 1 st knitwise, k2tog, psso.
Sssk Sl 3 sts knitwise one at a time to RH needle. Insert tip of LH needle into fronts of all 3 sts, and knit them together.
Dc3tog Double crochet 3 sts together.

〉 NOTES

1 When working RS rows, read chart from right to left; when working WS rows, read chart from left to right.
2 Place markers between the different charted pattern sts to help keep your place.

〉 SHAWL

Cast on 91 sts, and k 7 rows.

Beg chart

Row 1 (RS) Beg with first st, work to beg of 37-st rep, work 37-st rep twice, work to end of row.
Cont to foll chart in this way until piece measures approx 42"/106.5cm (or desired length without crochet border), end with a WS row.
(**Note** Crochet border adds approx 3"/7.6cm to each end.) Bind off.

〉 CROCHET BORDER

With WS facing, rejoin yarn to bound-off edge of wrap, and work as foll across 91 bound-off sts:
Row 1 Ch 3 (counts as 1 dc), dc in next st, *ch 2, skip 2 sts, dc in each of the next 3 sts; rep from * end, dc in next 2 sts. Turn.
Row 2 Ch 2 and dc in next st (counts as dc2tog over first 2 sts), *ch 4, skip ch-2 sp, dc3tog over next 3 dc; rep from * to end, end dc2tog instead of dc3tog. Turn.
Row 3 Ch 7 (counts as 1 dc and 4 ch), *dc in next dc3tog, ch 4; rep from * to end, dc in last dc2tog.
Row 4 Ch 1, sc in first dc, *7 tr in next dc, sc in next dc; rep from * to end, working last sc in 3rd ch of ch 7. Fasten off.
Work along cast-on edge the same way.

〉 FINISHING

Block piece flat to show lace patterns. ■

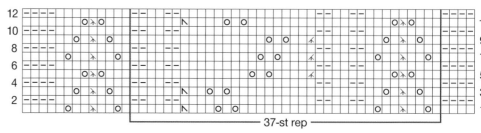

STITCH KEY

☐ k on RS, p on WS	◙ yarn over	◩ sssk
⊟ p on RS, k on WS	⊠ SK2P	⊡ k3tog

short-row feather scarf 〉〉〉

YARN

〉 3½oz/100g, 220yd/210m of any
worsted-weight silk blend yarn
in pale pink

NEEDLES

〉 One pair size 7 (4.5mm) needles
or size to obtain gauge

〉 MEASUREMENTS

Inside curve Approx 30"/76cm
Outside curve Approx 45"/114cm
Length at center Approx 5"/12.5cm

〉 GAUGE

14 sts and 28 rows to 4"/10cm over feather
faggoting st (lightly blocked) using size 7
(4.5mm) needles.
Take time to check your gauge.

〉 STITCH GLOSSARY

Feather fagotting st
(multiple of 4 plus 2)
Row 1 K1, *k1, yo, p2tog, k1; rep from * to
last st, sl 1 st purlwise.
Rep row 1 for feather fagotting st.

〉 SPECIAL TECHNIQUE

Short row wrap & turn
(w&t)
1 Work to specified st, wyif sl next st purlwise.
2 Move yarn between the needles to the back.
3 Sl the same st back to LH needle. Turn work.

〉 NOTE

Because of the stitch pattern, when working
the short rows with the w&t (wrap and turn)
method, it is not necessary to close up the
wraps when working over all the sts.

〉 SCARF

Cast on 106 sts. Work in feather fagotting st
for 5 rows.
Beg short row shaping
Next row (RS) Work in pat over 101 sts (or
5 sts from end of row), w&t.
Next row (WS) Work in pat over 96 sts (or
5 sts from end of row), w&t.
Next row (RS) Work in pat over 92 sts (or 9
sts from end of row), w&t.
Next row (WS) Work in pat over 88 sts (or
9 sts from end of row), w&t.
Cont in short rows, working 4 less sts at end
of every row, until 16 short rows have been
worked—there are 40 sts in center between
last wrapped sts on each side. After final
turn, work in pat to end of next row. Then
work next row in pat over all sts.

Beg increases

Inc row 1 (RS) K1, *k1, yo, p2tog, k1, yo, k1,
yo, p2tog, k1; rep from * to last st, sl 1—19 sts.
Inc row 2 K1, *k1, yo, p2tog, k1, yo, k2, yo,
p2tog, k1; rep from * to last st, sl 1—132 sts.
Inc row 3 K1, *k1, yo, p2tog, kfb, yo, p2tog,
kfb, yo, p2tog, k1; rep from * to last st, sl
1—158 sts. Work in pat for 10 rows. Bind off
sts loosely.

〉 FINISHING

Block pieces lightly to measurements. ■

Paul Amato for lvarepresents.com

simple triangle shawl »»

YARN ⑤

❯ 14oz/400g, 630yd/580m of any bulky-weight cotton blend ribbon yarn in variegated blue and brown

NEEDLES

❯ One size 10 (6mm) circular needle 29"/74cm long *or size to obtain gauge*

❯ MEASUREMENTS

Approx 62"/157.5cm wide x 40"/101.5cm at longest point

❯ GAUGE

13 sts and 20 rows to 4"/10cm over St st using size 10 (6mm) needle.
Take time to check your gauge.

❯ NOTE

A circular needle is used to accommodate the large number of sts. Do not join.

❯ SHAWL

Make a slipknot and place on needle.
Row 1 (RS) K1, yo, k1 into slipknot.
Row 2 Purl.
Row 3 K1, yo, k to last st, yo, k1.
Rep rows 2 and 3 until there are 201 sts.
Piece measures approx 62"/157.5cm wide and 40"/101.5cm (measured at center).
Loosely bind off all sts. ■

Jack Deutsch

openwork cowl 》》》

YARN

) 5¼oz/150g, 330yd/310m of any DK weight cotton blend yarn in light yellow

NEEDLES

) One pair size 6 (4mm) needles
or size to obtain gauge

》 MEASUREMENTS
Width Approx 6½"/16.5cm
Circumference Approx 44"/111.5cm

》 GAUGE
24 sts and 27 rows to 4"/10cm over pattern st using size 6 (4mm) needles.
Take time to check your gauge.

》 STITCH GLOSSARY
Pattern stitch
(multiple of 4 sts)
Row 1 (RS) *SKP, (yo) twice, k2tog; rep from * to end.
Row 2 *P1, (k1, p1) in double yo, p1; rep from * to end.
Rep rows 1 and 2 for pattern stitch.

》 COWL
Cast on 40 sts. Work in pat st until piece measures approx 44"/111.5cm from beg. Bind off.

》 FINISHING
Sew bound-off edge to cast-on edge. ■

Paul Amato for lvarepresents.com

spring lace scarf >>>

YARN ❷

) 7oz/200g, 680yd/630m of any sport weight wool and cotton blend yarn in blue

NEEDLES

) One pair size 7 (4.5mm) needles double-pointed needles (dpns) *or size to obtain gauge*

NOTIONS

) Stitch marker

) MEASUREMENTS

Approx 15 x 67"/38 x 70cm (without fringe)

) GAUGE

18 sts and 26 rows to 4"/10cm over lace pat using size 7 (4.5mm) needles after blocking. *Take time to check your gauge.*

) NOTE

Slip the first stitch of each row with yarn in front, then bring yarn to back between first and 2nd sts and knit.

) STITCH GLOSSARY

Lace pattern
(multiple of 4 sts)
Row 1 Sl 1, k3, *k2, yo, k2tog; rep from *to last 4 sts, end k3, k1 tbl.
Rep row 1 for lace pat.

) SCARF

Cast on 76 sts loosely.
Row 1 (WS) Sl 1 st, k to last st, k1 tbl.
Rows 2-7 Rep row 1.
Note Mark next row for RS.

Rose Callahan

Work in lace pat until piece measures 66¼"/168cm from beg.
Next 7 rows Work rows 1–7 same as beg of scarf. Bind off loosely.

) FINISHING

Block scarf.

Fringe
Cut 20½"/52cm lengths of yarn. Thread 4 strands through yarn needle; insert needle into edge stitch and pull yarn halfway through. Remove needle, line up ends of strands, then tie fringe into single knot close to edge of wrap. Tie one 4-strand fringe at each corner, and at each end of solid columns of sts. Tie 2 more knots in fringe at 2"/5cm apart. Trim ends of fringe to measure 2"/5cm below final knot. ■

grid stitch cowl >>>

YARN

> 7oz/200g, 460yd/420m of any DK weight wool yarn in pink

NEEDLES

> One size 5 (3.75mm) circular needle, 32"/80cm long *or size to obtain gauge*

NOTIONS

> Stitch marker

) MEASUREMENTS

Circumference Approx 35"/89cm
Width Approx 10½"/26.5cm

) GAUGE

23 sts and 38 rows to 4"/10cm over grid stitch using size 5 (3.75mm) needles. *Take time to check your gauge.*

) STITCH GLOSSARY

Grid stitch
(multiple of 5 sts)
Rnds 1, 3 and 5 Knit.
Rnds 2 and 4 *K4, p1; rep from * around.
Rnd 6 Purl.
Rep rnds 1–6 for grid stitch.

K1, p1 rib
(over an even number of sts)
Rnd 1 *K1, p1; rep from * around.
Rep rnd 1 for k1, p1 rib.

) COWL

Cast on 200 sts. Join, taking care not to twist sts. Place marker for beg of rnd and slip marker every rnd. Work in k1, p1 rib for 2 rnds. Work rnds 1–6 of grid st until cowl measures approx 10"/25.5cm from beg, end with a rnd 5. Work in k1, p1 rib for 2 rnds. Bind off loosely in rib. ■

Paul Amato for karenpresents.com

diamond lace stole >>>

YARN ②

> 5¼oz/150g, 530yd/490m of any sport weight cotton yarn in light blue

NEEDLES

> One pair size 5 (3.75mm) needles *or size to obtain gauge*

> ◼◼◼◻

〉 MEASUREMENTS

Approx 11 x 57"/28 x 144.5cm

〉 GAUGE

26 sts and 30 rows to 4"/10cm over St st using size 5 (3.75mm) needles.
Take time to check your gauge.

〉 SCARF

Cast on 67 sts.
Row 1 (WS) Knit.
Row 2 K2, *SKP, yo; rep from * to last 3 sts, k3.
Rows 3–5 Knit.

Beg chart

Work rows 1–42 of chart 10 times.
Next row (RS) K2, k2tog, yo, k5, k2tog, yo, k6, yo, SKP, k13, yo, SK2P, yo, k13, k2tog, yo, k6, yo, SKP, k5, yo, SKP, k2.
Next row (WS) Knit.
Next row (RS) K2, *SKP, yo; rep from * to last 3 sts, k3.
Knit 3 rows.
Bind off.

〉 FINISHING

Block lightly. ◼

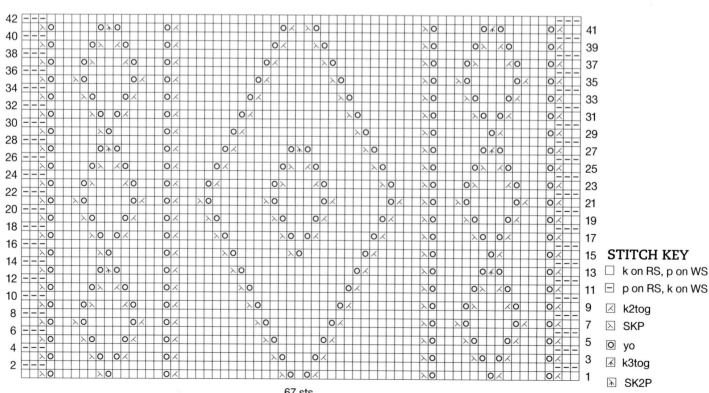

67 sts

STITCH KEY

☐ k on RS, p on WS

⊟ p on RS, k on WS

⊠ k2tog

⊠ SKP

◎ yo

⊠ k3tog

⊠ SK2P

skinny summer scarf 》》》

YARN

》 3½oz/100g, 240yd/220m of any
DK weight cotton blend yarn in
either orange, dark pink, light pink,
or medium blue

NEEDLES

》 One pair size 7 (4.5mm) needles
or size to obtain gauge

》 MEASUREMENTS

Approx 4½ x 60"/11.5 x 152cm

》 GAUGE

20 sts and 32 rows to 4"/10cm over pat
using size 7 (4.5mm) needles.
Take time to check your gauge.

》 SCARF

Cast on 23 sts.
Row 1 (RS) K2, p2, [k3, p3] twice, k3, p2, k2.
Row 2 K4, [p3, k3] twice, p3, k4.
Row 3 Rep row 1.
Rows 4 and 6 K4, [p3, k3] twice, p3, k4.
Row 5 K2, p2, [k3, p3] twice, k3, p2, k2.
Row 7 K4, [yo, SK2P, yo, k3] twice, yo, SK2P,
yo, k4.
Rows 8 and 10 K2, p2, [k3, p3] twice, k3,
p2, k2.
Row 9 K4, [p3, k3] twice, p3, k4.
Row 11 K2, k2tog, [yo, k3, yo, SK2P] twice,
yo, k3, yo, SKP, k2.
Rep rows 4–11 until piece measures
59½"/151cm from beg, end with a row 5.
Rep rows 4–6 once more. Bind off. ■

Paul Amato for lvarepresents.com